SONIA SOTOMAYOR

First Latina Supreme Court Justice

SONIA SOTOMAYOR

First Latina Supreme Court Justice

John Torres

Enslow Publishing
101 W. 23rd Street
Suite 240
New York, NY 10011
USA

enslow.com

Published in 2016 by Enslow Publishing, LLC
101 W. 23rd Street, Suite 240, New York, NY 10011

Library of Congress Cataloging-in-Publication Data
Torres, John, author.
Sonia Sotomayor : first Latina Supreme Court Justice / John Torres.
    pages cm. — (Influential Latinos)
Includes bibliographical references and index.
Summary: "Discusses the life and work of Sonia Sotomayor"—Provided by publisher.
ISBN 978-0-7660-7001-1
1. Sotomayor, Sonia, 1954—Juvenile literature. 2. Hispanic American judges—Biography—Juvenile literature. 3. Judges—United States—Biography—Juvenile literature. 4. United States. Supreme Court—Biography—Juvenile literature. I. Title.
KF8745.S67T67 2016
347.73'2634—dc23
[B]
                                2015012781

Printed in the United States of America

To Our Readers: We have done our best to make sure all Web site addresses in this book were active and appropriate when we went to press. However, the author and the publisher have no control over and assume no liability for the material available on those Web sites or on any Web sites they may link to. Any comments or suggestions can be sent by e-mail to customerservice@enslow.com.

Photo Credits: Abby Brack/Getty Images Entertainment/Getty Images, p. 108; Alain Le Garsmeur/ Hulton Archive/Getty Images, p. 81; Alex Wong/Getty Images News/Getty Images, p. 94; Allison Shelley/Getty Images news/Getty Images, p. 103; © AP Images, p. 69; Barbara Alper/Archive Photos/Getty Images, p. 74; Bill Turnbull/NY Daily News Archive via Getty Images, p. 58; Bruce Glikas/ FilmMagic/Getty Images, p. 115; CBS Photo Archive via Getty Images, p. 49; Chip Somodevilla/ Getty Images News/Getty Images, p. 17; courtesy of the Everett Collection, p. 16; D Dipasupil/Getty Images Entertainment/Getty Images, p. 52; Dmitry Lobanov/Shutterstock.com, p. 45; George Napolitano/FilmMagic/Getty Images, p. 96; Joshua Roberts/Bloomberg via Getty Images, pp. 10, 77; J. SCOTT APPLEWHITE/AFP/Getty Images, p. 86; Kanus/ullstein bild via Getty Images, p. 39; Laura Cavanaugh/FilmMagic/Getty Images, p. 111; Marie Hansen/The LIFE Picture Collection/ Getty Images, p. 27; Mark Wilson/Getty Images News/Getty Images, pp. 3, 6, 116; PAUL J. RICH-ARDS/AFP/Getty Images, p. 12; Pete Souza/The White House via Getty Images, p. 8; Pete Spiro/ Shutterstock.com, pp. 60, 64; Photo12/UIG via Getty Images, p. 23; rnl/Shutterstock.com, p. 59; Ron Galella/WireImage/Getty Images, p. 71; Spencer Platt/Getty Images News/Getty Images, pp. 105, 117; The White House via Getty Images, pp. 14, 33; Tim Mosenfelder/Hulton Archive/Getty Images, p. 89; Tom Lynn/Sports Illustrated/Getty Images, p. 100; Topical Press Agency/Hulton Archive/ Getty Images, p. 20; Veronica Louro/Shutterstock.com, p. 79; © White House Press Office/Zuma-press.com, pp. 30, 42, 55.

Cover Credit: Mark Wilson/Getty Images News/Getty Images (Sonia Sotomayor).

Contents

Sonia Sotomayor is the first person of Hispanic descent to be appointed to the US Supreme Court.

Chapter 1

AMERICAN DREAM COME TRUE

S onia Sotomayor could barely contain her happiness, or for that matter, her smile. It went from ear to ear, like a child's on Christmas morning. She was standing next to the president of the United States, Barack Obama, and Vice President Joe Biden. Obama leaned over and whispered something in her ear about not being nervous.

The president moved to the microphone and made the announcement that would change Sotomayor's life forever. On this day, May 26, 2009, she would become part of history and her childhood dreams would come true.

"Of the many responsibilities granted to a President by our Constitution, few are more serious or more consequential than selecting a Supreme Court justice,"

Sotomayor meets with Barack Obama, the president who appointed her to the Supreme Court.

the president began. "So I don't take this decision lightly. I've made it only after deep reflection and careful deliberation.... After completing this exhaustive process, I have decided to nominate an inspiring woman who I believe will make a great justice: Judge Sonia Sotomayor of the great state of New York."[1]

Interviewed by the President

It was only a week earlier that the president summoned Sotomayor to the White House to meet with her about the possibility. She had been serving as a judge on the US Appellate Court for the previous 10 years and had earned the reputation as a hard-working and fearless judge, who was not afraid of making her own decisions and speaking her mind.

That toughness came from years of determination to make a career for herself during a time in the United States when women were still expected to take jobs as teachers and nurses instead of doctors and lawyers. That toughness came from having to prove to herself and her classmates that she belonged at Princeton University during a time when not many Hispanic women were being admitted to the college. That toughness came from years as a prosecutor on the tough streets of New York City where she worked tirelessly to put criminals behind bars, often looking for witnesses herself in dangerous, crime-riddled neighborhoods.

During the interview, President Obama was very impressed by her life story and how hard she had to work to make it to where she was today. Much like his own story, Sotomayor had to overcome many obstacles in her early life. He liked that grit and determination and four days later he placed a phone call to Sotomayor letting her know that he was planning to nominate her for the open position on the US Supreme Court—the highest court in the country. "She is, in a way, a counterpart of Obama himself . . . It's the American Dream—anybody can make it," one of Sotomayor's former bosses, George Parvia told the *Washington Post*.[2]

It was no secret that the 54-year-old woman of Puerto Rican descent was being considered. There was a short list of four or five judges that the president was

Sotomayor is sworn in for her confirmation hearings in 2009. She was nominated to fill the vacancy left by David Souter.

considering for the replacement of Justice David Souter, who was retiring. In fact, a couple of US senators had already written letters to President Obama, urging him to select Sotomayor to the post.

Still, it came as a welcome shock and surprise when the president called her to say he had made his decision. For the next day and a half, the smile never left her lips. "I was in total disbelief when he called me that day," she told television personality Oprah Winfrey. "I don't cry but the tears just started coming down my face and my heart was beating so hard that I actually thought he could hear my heart. It was the most electrifying moment of my life. It was an overwhelming moment."[3] She held the telephone in one hand and placed her other hand over her heart to quiet it down.

Accepting the Nomination

After the president introduced her as his choice, Sotomayor approached the microphone and accepted the nomination with her typical humility and grace. "Thank you Mr. President for the most humbling honor of my life. I could not, could not, in the few minutes I have today, mention the names of the many friends and family who have guided and supported me throughout my life, and who have been instrumental in helping me realize my dreams. I see many of the faces in this room. Each of you, whom I love deeply, will know that my heart today is bursting with gratitude for all you have done for me."[4]

Sotomayor is sworn in by Chief Justice John Roberts in the East Conference room of the Supreme Court on August 8, 2009. Her mother and brother were present to witness the swearing in.

She went on to acknowledge her relatives and friends in attendance but saved the most important for last.

> *I stand on the shoulders of countless people, yet there is one extraordinary person who is my life aspiration. That person is my mother, Celina Sotomayor. My mother has devoted her life to my brother and me. And as the President mentioned, she worked often two jobs to help support us after dad died. I have often said that I am all I am because of her, and I am only half the woman she is.*[5]

During her short acceptance speech, Sotomayor recalled her first visit to the While House only 11 years earlier and what the nomination to the highest court in the land meant to her now. "It is a daunting feeling to be

Barack Obama

While Sonia Sotomayor made history as the first Hispanic US Supreme Court Justice, the man who appointed her to the post made similar history a few years earlier. US President Barrack Obama made history on January 20, 2009 when—during an ice-cold outdoor ceremony—he was sworn in as the forty-fourth president of the United States. The historic part? Well, he is the first African-American man to be elected president of the country. His story is very similar in ways to that of Justice Sotomayor.

Obama was born on August 4, 1961 in Hawaii. His mother, who is white, was from Kansas and his father was from the African nation of Kenya. His parents divorced when he was very young and moved to the country of Indonesia for a few years as his mother continued her studies and her career there. Later he moved back to Hawaii and was raised mainly by his mother and his grandparents.

He worked throughout college to help pay for his studies at Columbia University, an Ivy League School. He also relied on scholarships and student loans. He decided to attend law school and attended Harvard University, where he became the first African-American president of the *Harvard Law Review*.

He was elected to the Illinois State Senate and then later made the jump to the US Senate before running for the presidency. He was elected to a second term in 2012. President Obama is married to Michelle Obama. The couple are raising two daughters, Malia and Sasha.

Judge Sonia Sotomayor poses with her mother Celina Sotomayor on the day Sonia was announced as a nominee to the United States Supreme Court.

here. Eleven years ago, during my confirmation process for appointment to the Second Circuit, I was given a private tour of the White House. It was an overwhelming experience for a kid from the South Bronx," she said. "Yet never in my wildest childhood imaginings did I ever envision that moment, let alone did I ever dream that I would live this moment. … I am an ordinary person who has been blessed with extraordinary opportunities and experiences. Today is one of those experiences."[6]

The Confirmation Process

What followed was known as the confirmation process. That is when nominees to such positions are questioned by members of Congress about everything in their past. They also examined every one of Sonia's rulings as a judge, her speeches, and personal life to make sure she was a good fit.

The process took a few months, but in early August the US Senate was set to vote on whether to accept the president's nomination or tell him to select someone else. Sotomayor watched the hearings on television in her private chambers of the New York courthouse where she worked as an appellate judge. The final tally was 68–31. And suddenly, the little girl who went to bed reading Nancy Drew novels and dreaming of becoming a detective and then a lawyer, had been named a justice on the US Supreme Court.

When she arrived home that night to her small apartment in New York City's West Village, her neighbors had lined the streets to welcome her home. She smiled broadly and waved as her neighbors and friends applauded and called her name.

In a few days she would be sworn in as the third woman to ever serve on the Supreme Court and the first Hispanic. She will hold the position until she wishes to retire.

Hers is a story made for Hollywood: The poor, sickly girl raised by a single mother who stressed education to her two children, who manages to make it to two of the

Nancy Drew

Nancy Drew is a fictional character created by a publisher in the 1930s for a series of books called "The Nancy Drew Mystery Stories." Several authors worked on the series but were not given writing credit. Instead, the books

say they are written by Carolyn Keene. The series lasted until 2004 when a new series called "Girl Detective" was started that featured a modernized version of the young crime solver. That series ended in 2013 when the "Nancy Drew Files," series was started.

Nancy is a teenaged high school graduate who lives in the fictional town of River Heights. She is raised only by her father, a lawyer, and their housekeeper. In the books, Nancy spends her time solving mysteries that she comes across accidentally or that her father is connected to as a lawyer. Her family is very wealthy and in some adventures she gets to travel all over the world solving mysteries in exotic locations. She sometimes is joined by her close friends and in some of the stories she has a boyfriend.

Her stories have been made into movies and television shows and her appeal has been to young girls worldwide who love to read her stories. Nancy Drew remains wildly popular and has been credited with inspiring people like Sonia Sotomayor and Hillary Clinton. The original publisher, Edward Stratemeyer, created a similar series to appeal to boys called the "Hardy Boys Mysteries."

President Obama welcomed Sotomayor to the Supreme Court during a reception he hosted in her honor.

best universities in the country and follows her dream. But for anyone who digs deeper, or who knows Sonia Sotomayor, there is so much more to her story and her dream than simply being successful. "I have found satisfaction in my life through my work but it alone has not given me success or happiness," she said during a speech at Pace University in White Plains, New York.

> Passion in pursuing a dream and in doing good in the world is a wonderful goal. It is a goal you will not find satisfying in reaching, however, without recognizing that the more important part of life is your connection with the people whom you travel the journey of your life with. Also important is the quality of sharing and giving that you do in your life.[7]

Sotomayor has always been about justice and wanting to be a voice to the voiceless, the poor, and the underprivileged. She has never tolerated bullies and has always taken sides with the underdog. As she said in her speech, true happiness comes from "doing good."

This is her story.

Chapter 2

WAR CHANGES DESTINIES

One would be hard-pressed to find two communities farther apart on the small island of Puerto Rico than the areas of Santurce and Lajas. The first, Santurce, is at the northeast part of the island and is the most populated part of the vibrant, bustling capital of San Juan. Lajas, a quiet rural area located near the southwest coast, isn't really close to any major cities.

The driving distance today is about two hours. It was a lot longer back in the 1920s when Sonia Sotomayor's parents were born. Her father, Juan Sotomayor was born in 1921 in Santurce. Her mother Celina Baez was born in 1927.

Lajas has become a popular tourist destination over the years but back in 1927 it was little more than a fishing village once settled by Spanish Jews. There was little reason or opportunity for people from Lajas or Santurce to interact with each other back then. They might have been worlds apart.

Puerto Rico was much more provincial when Sonia Sotomayor's parents were growing up there.

Celina Sotomayor

It took a world war, sad childhoods, and a journey of thousands of miles for Sotomayor's parents to meet. But it's important to figure out first why anyone would ever choose to leave a lush tropical paradise and move so far away to a strange land where the people spoke a different language. For Sonia Sotomayor, her journey from Bronx schoolgirl to the US Supreme Court can be best understood and appreciated by starting with her parents.

Her mother Celina had a very sad and lonely childhood. Her father abandoned her when she was born and her mother suffered from a terrible mental and physical illness. She had to stay in bed most of the time and was unable to care for herself. Sometimes her mother would go wandering and get lost, having to be brought back home by the many family members that shared their tiny country home.

Because of her mother's sickness, Celina was raised by her older brothers and sisters. She worked, even as a young child, sewing handkerchiefs and other items for ladies in order to help the family earn enough money.

She loved reading and looked forward to quiet time at the end of the night even though she was normally exhausted from traveling a very far distance to school every day, sewing her handkerchiefs and doing her daily chores. She found magic in the words and couldn't read the stories she loved fast enough.

When she was only nine years old Celina's mother died. This changed things drastically for the family as they basically moved away from the family home in Lajas. Celina would move with her oldest sister, Aurora and her husband to a town called San German.

She continued her studies, as well as her sewing but something had changed. In San German she could see that only the wealthier girls were the ones who went off to college and that there were not very many opportunities for a poor country girl like her who had no parents.

Around this time, Japan had attacked the US Naval base at Pearl Harbor and suddenly the country was getting ready to fight the Germans and the Japanese in World War II. Puerto Rico is a Caribbean island that is known as a commonwealth territory of the United States, meaning it is US property that comes with certain privileges while at the same time maintaining a bit of independence in certain matters. Anyone born in Puerto Rico is automatically a US citizen. During this time, Puerto Rico was simply known as a US territory.

Many of the island's young men began enlisting in the US Army to go and fight in the war. This inspired Celina greatly. She also saw it as a possible way of escaping her fate as a poor country girl. While women were not allowed to join the regular armed forces back then as they are now, there was a special branch known as the Women's Army Corps or WACs.

Only seventeen at the time, Celina lied about her age and signed up. It was a six-hour train ride from San

When Japan destroyed US Navy boats in an attack on Pearl Harbor,
Celina was enlisted in the US Women's Army Corps.

German to San Juan where she was told to report for a physical exam and other tests. She did well and somehow produced a fake birth certificate saying she was nineteen years old.

Before long she was on a plane to Miami and then to Georgia for basic training. The work was hard for someone who had never used a telephone and was not used to the technology available in this modern world. She also had to learn basic English skills almost overnight. Her commanding officers only spoke English so if she didn't want to get into trouble she would have to learn what they were saying. Everything was different and difficult but Celina could not have been happier.

Her life had gone from being one long chore to suddenly becoming an adventure. She had escaped the drudgery and loneliness of her life. Even though she had been raised by other family members, mainly her brothers and sisters, Celina always felt like an orphan.

After basic training, she was stationed in New York, where her job was to help sort letters at the main post office for the soldiers that were fighting overseas. The job of the WACs was basically to do the things that men normally did so that more of them could go and fight in the war.

They all lived together in a hotel in New York City. Eventually Celina started making friends and enjoying life in the big city including dinner shows, concerts, and movies. It was after news broke of Germany's surrender that Celina and a friend went to a big party in the Bronx.

Women's Army Auxiliary Corps

Many female volunteers assisted the army overseas during World War I, mainly by working telephones, cooking, and serving food. But because they were not affiliated with the Army in an official capacity, they had to find their own food and place to sleep.

Before the United States became involved in World War II, Congresswoman Edith Nourse Rogers proposed a bill that would start the Women's Army Auxiliary Corps. Later it would be shortened to the Women's Army Corps. Her idea was not taken seriously until the Japanese bombed Pearl Harbor in December, 1941.

It wasn't long after that Congress passed the bill that was signed into law by President Franklin D. Roosevelt that the WAAC had achieved its goal of 150,000 women. Some of the jobs they were trained for and performed during war included things like drivers, weather forecasters, car and plane repairs, radio operators, making bullets and bombs, and other important tasks.

The philosophy behind the organization was that for every woman who worked doing these jobs it would allow another American man to go to war and defend the country. General Douglas MacArthur once called the WACs "his best soldiers." Some women joined because they had lost their husbands in the war. Others joined because no one in their family was able to go and fight and so they wanted to do their part for the war effort.

The WAC program was discontinued in 1978. Today, women are allowed to enter every branch of the armed forces and participate in combat.

That was where she would meet her future husband and Sonia's father, Juan Luis Sotomayor, whose nickname was "Juli." The pair hit it off right away and shared a similar story.

Juan Sotomayor

Juan too had loved school and was a very good student, showing a gift for mathematic calculations. In fact, college officials heard about his math skills and offered to send him to the university at a young age but his mother said she did not want him to go and that became the end of that. When his father became very sick with tuberculosis, Juan had to quit school in the sixth grade and start working in a button factory to help support his family. He was the oldest child and when his father died from the disease it became his duty to provide for his mother and his siblings.

When the war started he tried to enlist in the armed forces as well but doctors discovered a heart problem and would not let him serve. Still, his mother decided to move the family to New York and start a new life there and look for opportunities that did not exist in Puerto Rico at that time.

His work options were limited. There wasn't much he was qualified for. Juan only had a sixth-grade education and could not speak any English. Still, he found work in a mannequin factory, where he taught himself how to sculpt. According to Sonia's biography, *My Beloved World*, he would create realistic busts of

The Women's Army Corps (WAC) was the women's branch of the US Army.

famous historical figures based on their photographs in the newspaper. He would even create one of Celina.

He became very depressed when the mannequin factory closed down but he was a hard worker and soon found a job at a radiator factory where he would sometimes help out with the accounting and book keeping because he was so good at math.

Newlyweds

Juan and Celina fell in love and when her deployment with the Women's Army Corps ended she had the option of returning to Puerto Rico, a little more educated and a lot worldlier than when she departed the island. But that was never really an option. In fact, Celina viewed her upbringing as so harsh that she wanted to continue her new life in the United States.

Juan asked her to marry him and the two went to city hall and became husband and wife.

At first everything was wonderful. Celina was accepted into Juan's large family. Unlike her own, Juan's family seemed very happy and enjoyed parties, dancing, storytelling, and having a good time. The happy couple lived downstairs from his family in an old building and Juan encouraged Celina to continue her education, knowing how important it was to her. So, during their first few years of marriage, Celina went back to school, finished high school, took secretarial classes, and then even went to school to later become a practical nurse.

Life was perfect. Celina was now part of a large, extended family and there always seemed to be a party that went long and late into the night. What Celina did not know, what she could not have known was that behind the dancing, the storytelling, the parties and the smiles, Juan had never gotten over his father's death when he was 13 and his mother's subsequent remarriage. He started drinking alcohol at a young age and slowly, over time, it would nearly destroy everything.

Juan and Celina Sotomayor welcomed their first child, Sonia, in 1954.
The young family didn't have much, but they were happy.

Chapter 3

HUMBLE BEGINNINGS

hile Celina Sotomayor was furthering her education, she and her husband Juan were also trying to have a family. It took them seven years to conceive a child. Finally, their patience was rewarded on June 25, 1954 with the birth of their first child and future US Supreme Court Justice, Sonia Marie Sotomayor.

Even though Juan was not a very educated man, he must have remembered the opportunities that he once had and was very supportive of his wife going to school and learning as much as she could. This was not common during that time period. Women, especially Latin women, were not expected to go to school and work. Rather, in many households they were expected to be housewives, staying home with the children, cleaning the house, and cooking dinner.

But it was Celina's education and zest for knowledge that would inspire her daughter and one-day Supreme Court Justice.

Sonia would not be an only child for very long. About three years after her birth, her parents gave her a brother, Juan—named after his father.

Bronxdale Houses

By this time, the children's mother was working as a telephone operator at small, private hospital in the South Bronx and the family was able to move from their South Bronx tenement to the Bronxdale Houses, a housing project located a short drive away from their old neighborhood.

Most housing projects—apartments dedicated to the poor—are typically not very safe or very nice places to live. But the Bronxdale Houses were fairly new, racially mixed, and considered one of the better city housing projects to live in. Many families tried to move there and eventually there was a waiting list.

Even though it was one of the better ones, there were still problems. During an interview in 1988 with the Associated Press, Sotomayor said she witnessed many kids make the wrong choices while living there:

> *There were working poor in the projects. There were poor poor in the projects. There were sick poor in the projects. There were addicts and non-addicts and all sorts of people, every one of them with problems, and each group with a different response, different methods*

Not long after Sonia's baby brother, Juan, was born, the Sotomayors moved Into the Bronxdale Houses.

of survival, different reactions to the adversity they were facing. And you saw kids making choices."

The move, however, was not a happy one for the entire extended family. While the Bronxdale Houses were a safer and nicer place for Juan and Celina to raise their children, it was also the first time they ever lived apart from Juan's mother and his brothers, sisters, and cousins. There had been a large family support system that now was no longer there.

It also took Juan away from a neighborhood that he had known and loved for a long time. Even though his family would eventually follow them and move into the same neighborhood, Juan became more depressed and started drinking more. By this time, his drinking had become so bad that he hardly left the apartment except to go to work and to take Sonia to the grocery store with him once a week to buy food. He rarely ever attended the family parties that were once so much fun for everyone.

Emphasis on Education

Like many other children whose parents migrated from Puerto Rico, Sonia attended Catholic school. Traditionally, Latino families have traditionally preferred religious schools to public institutions, believing their children would get a better education there and a better chance at a good career and a way out of poverty. But Catholic schools can be expensive and this meant that parents sometimes held down two jobs in order to send their children to these schools.

Puerto Rican Migration

Puerto Ricans did not start leaving the island and moving to the mainland United States in large numbers until there was a terrible economic depression very early in the twentieth century. According to the Library of Congress, in 1910, there were less than 2,000 Puerto Ricans living on the mainland, mainly in New York City. By 1930 that number had grown to more than 40,000. The big influx of Puerto Ricans from the island to the mainland however occurred right around the time Sonia Sotomayor's mother and father moved to New York, right after World War II ended.

There were several reasons for the sudden and drastic increase in numbers. The first is that the economy in Puerto Rico was still doing poorly and there were not many jobs. Second, family members who had already established themselves in the United States were now urging family members to make the move as well. Another reason is that many of the soldiers and WACs who served during the war were not interested in going back to the island after they had seen the world.

The migration continued to grow throughout the 1950s and 1960s. Today there are nearly 5 million Puerto Ricans residing in the 50 states—the majority staying in big cities like New York, Chicago, Boston, Philadelphia, and Orlando, according to the US Census Bureau. Many of them, like Sonia Sotomayor, are second-generation Puerto Ricans, having been born on the mainland.

Sonia, and many of her close friends from the Bronxdale Houses, attended Blessed Sacrament Catholic School when she was in elementary school. She didn't like the strict rules and the harsh punishments the nuns would sometimes impose on her and her classmates. She felt the nuns did not approve of Sonia's mother working, even though there was no way she would be able to afford attending the school if her mother didn't work. None of Sonia's cousins went to Catholic school; all of them attended public schools.

It was while Sonia and her brother were still very young that her mother, Celina, realized that the only way her children were going to advance and make it out of the projects one day and make a better living than she and Juan was through education. She stressed schoolwork and studies to her children, even from a very young age and even started doing something that most people in the projects could not afford in addition to sending her children to Catholic school—she started buying her children an encyclopedia set. The books would come one or two every month and were quite expensive.

Before the Internet, this was how most people did research. The sets of books, often twenty-four or twenty-six to a collection would contain articles about everything from history to sports to entertainment to pop culture and geography. It was sort of like having the information available on Google in a set of books.

Visiting Puerto Rico

Celina was working nights now as a nurse in the hospital and Juan would make the children dinner and take care of them after he returned from work. But his drinking was getting worse and his health started to fail. He was getting sick a lot and his hands would even shake

The Commonwealth of Puerto Rico

Puerto Rico, as you've read so far, is a commonwealth of the US It's not a state, it's not a colony, so exactly what does it mean to be a commonwealth?

There are two areas that are commonwealth territories of the United States. One is, of course, Puerto Rico, and the other are the Northern Mariana Islands. It is interesting to note that both territories have very different relationships with the United States.

Anyone born in Puerto Rico is an American citizen. Puerto Rico has its own government with its own elected officials, but at the same time has a nonvoting representative in the US House of Representatives—one of the branches of Congress. The people of the island receive protection and benefits of being American citizens yet do not pay Federal taxes if they live in Puerto Rico. They are also unable to vote in American presidential elections.

Every few years the people of Puerto Rico hold a non-binding vote, meant really as a message to the American government—regarding their commonwealth status. The people can choose to become a state, become totally independent, or remain a commonwealth, which continues to be what the people want, though more and more people over the years are voting for Puerto Rico to become a state.

when he didn't have a drink. It caused many arguments in the house and Sonia looked for any excuse to get away, whether it was to the park or a sleepover at her grandmother's house.

Despite being born in New York, Sonia's family never wanted her to forget her roots. As a result, some of her earliest and nicest memories are of trips to Puerto Rico as child. Sometimes she would travel with just her grandmother—Juan's mother—and later on she would travel there with her own mother. Celina, who had a miserably unhappy childhood, had vowed never to go back. But as time passed, the bad feelings went away and she eventually returned to the island.

In her biography, *My Beloved World*, Sonia recounts the wonderful experiences she had on trips to Puerto Rico with her mother. "Some of the best summer vacations I remember were traveling with my mother and Junior to Mayaguez to visit her family," she wrote, adding that her mother had barely travelled out of her own neighborhood as a child and was now eager to explore the island. "She was eager to show us places that she'd heard about but had never seen herself."[2]

They would visit museums, relatives, cities and historical sites, and sample just about every new food they could. Sonia was drawn to the sweet desserts and fruits like mangoes. No one saw this as a warning at the time, but it would soon cause a major health concern for a little girl who was destined for greatness.

Juan and Celina wanted their children to connect with their heritage. Sonia loved traveling to Puerto Rico to explore the island.

A few years later, before Sonia turned eight years old, she was attending mass, or church service, at Blessed Sacrament when suddenly everything went black. She had passed out, fainted. When she finally opened her eyes, all of the nuns were gathered around her with worried, anxious looks on their faces.

Celina rushed her daughter to the hospital and the doctors performed a few tests before confirming that Sonia suffered from type 1 diabetes. When the doctors told her mother, she started to cry. It was the first time Sonia had ever seen her mother cry and it made her very nervous. But the doctor explained to Sonia that even though things were serious, she could live a long, happy, and normal life. Diabetes, he explained, is a dangerous, deadly disease in which the body stops producing a chemical called insulin that the blood needs to break down or process the sugar that we eat. Sonia's life had changed forever in an instant. She would need an insulin injection every day for the rest of her life.

Chapter 4

It is true that Sonia's life changed the day she was diagnosed with diabetes. It is a disease she will have to live with for the rest of her life, constantly testing the sugar level in her blood and giving herself injections. But sometimes life is not fair, and something even worse would happen to Sonia and her family before she turned ten years of age.

Changes to the Sotomayor Family

It was an April afternoon and Sonia was walking home from school, a very short walk from the projects where she lived. On that day, there was no need to go to the babysitter who watched her and her brother for a few hours every day until her father got home from work because her father was home. He had not been feeling well and stayed home sick that day. In fact, he had not been doing well for a while. Juan Sotomayor was skinny and frail. He didn't seem to have the energy that he once had.

Sonia's life would change drastically with the tragic death of her father. Suddenly she found herself taking charge of the family.

Sonia knew something was wrong the instant she neared the door to her apartment and could hear voices, lots of them. She recognized aunts, cousins, and friends of the family. Buy why would so many people be inside her apartment in the middle of a weekday afternoon? She got her answer the second she opened the door and saw that just about everyone was crying or had red, swollen eyes because they had been crying. Something terrible must have happened. But what?

She looked around the room full of people and saw her mother sitting in a chair crying and her heart sank. "God has taken him," she told her daughter, and that was the exact moment that Sonia knew for sure that her father had died. Juan Sotomayor was only forty-two years old when he passed away from complications having to do with a bad heart and acute alcoholism. The pain of losing his own father at a young age had caused him to start drinking and he was never able to stop.

Celina was suddenly a thirty-six-year-old widow with two young children that she would have to provide for all by herself. This was still during a period of history —the 1960s—where women were not expected to work and it was rare to see a woman raising children by herself.

Changes started happening quickly. The family, too upset and saddened to keep living in the same apartment where Juan died, moved into another unit of the Bronxdale Houses. Celina explained her situation at work and was no longer required to work nights. This way, she was able to spend her evenings with the children, making them dinner and helping them with their homework.

But there were other changes that were not good. Juan's family grew distant from Celina and the once-happy very large family now felt empty. The parties and the dancing and the late-night poetry reading had ended. Everyone felt a little guilty for never doing anything to help Juan quit drinking the alcohol that was slowly killing him.

Celina's heart was also empty now. She fell slowly and deeply into a depression and did not know how to handle it. She spent hours locked in her bedroom in silence. She kept the apartment dark with all the lights turned off and the curtains drawn. After work she would make and serve dinner and then disappear into the darkness and quiet of her bedroom. Sonia had to take on more responsibilities and helped her brother with his homework at night. Their only company was watching television. It was very hard on the children to understand what was going on in their world.

Sonia Takes Control

It was worse for Sonia and her brother in the summer. At least when school was in session she had her studies and assignments to occupy her mind. Now, in the summer, there was really nothing to take her mind off her mother and her misery. Part of her wanted to go outside and play with her friends but a bigger part wanted her to stay close to home. Maybe she was afraid that her mother would die as well.

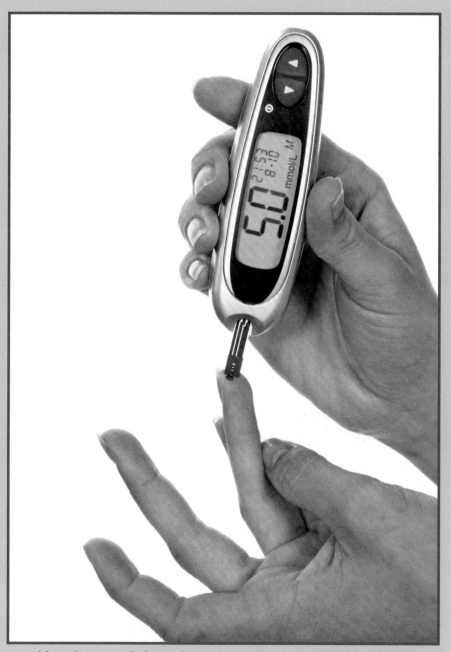

Although Sonia's diabetes diagnosis requires a daily insulin injection and regular blood sugar checks, the disease is managable.

So that summer was when Sonia discovered just how much she loved to read. She had always been a good reader and enjoyed it, but this summer was different. This summer she tore through books at the neighborhood library and found a new favorite topic to read about: Greek mythology.

She loved how the gods and goddesses would meddle in people's lives. But she also loved how ordinary people had to take charge of their own lives. And that is what Sonia did. For example, that Christmas, she went out with her brother and picked out a Christmas tree. She even put the lights on herself, fixed the skirt around the tree, and set up the Nativity scene.

And after getting sick and tired of seeing her mother waste away in sadness, she decided it was time to take charge of her own life. She banged on her mother's door and started yelling in a way that she had never done before. She told her mother that her father had died and she didn't want to see her mother die too. It was time to snap out of this terrible depression and start living once more. Before she knew it, Sonia was screaming and crying. She ran to her room and collapsed on her bed for the night.

Things Begin to Look Up

The next day her mother was a different person. She had come out of her fog and her mourning and started being what Sonia and her brother needed most—a real mother. She was making meals, cleaning the house, and

Greek Mythology

Just about every ancient civilization came up with explanations for the sun, wind, rain, and other parts of our world including men, women, animals, and even love. But one can argue that no one did it as interestingly or as with as much flair as they did in ancient Greece. Traces of Greek mythology can be seen today in comic book superheroes and in movies.

The earliest and most popular stories were written by a poet named Homer. In his classic tales *The Odyssey* and *The Iliad* the gods and goddesses meddle in the lives of ordinary men. The stories are often centered on Mount Olympus where the gods and goddesses lived ruled by Zeus. Most of the gods in the stories had one particular power or responsibility. For example, some of the better-known gods include Athena, who was the goddess of wisdom; Ares, who was the god of war; Aphrodite, who was the goddess of love; and Poseidon, who ruled the seas. If someone in the stories fell in love, the people knew it was the work of Aphrodite. If there was a tidal wave in the ocean, then the people knew that Poseidon was angry.

The US space program was influenced by Greek mythology in naming some of its vehicles and missions in the past, like Apollo. The stories are still popular today in video games, movies, and books. The popular series of books for young readers: "Percy Jackson and the Olympians" features a boy in modern times—Percy—who is the son of Poseidon.

taking care of things. Suddenly, Sonia did not have to do the things normally handled by grownups.

It allowed her to be a kid, and more importantly, a student. She immersed herself in her schoolwork and learned better study habits. Things soon began changing at school. The nuns no longer seemed so harsh and the work started coming a little easier. Sonia now felt as if she was one of the smarter children in her class instead of the girl who always seemed to be struggling. She liked the way it made her feel.

Her mother signed Sonia up for ballet class, piano and guitar lessons in an effort to help expand her education. But it was those encyclopedias that arrived one a month that transported Sonia to other worlds that involved science, geography, history, and nature. In her autobiography, Sotomayor describes receiving the books each month as "Christmas come early."

Career Ambition

With her newfound confidence and improving grades, Sonia began daydreaming about what she would be when she got older. The answer came from nowhere else but some of her favorite books: *The Nancy Drew Mysteries.*

Nancy Drew was a fictional character is a series of books that solved crimes. Sonia saved reading her Nancy Drew stories for right before bed. She did this on purpose, hoping to continue the adventures in her dreams, which she often did. She would become a detective and make the streets safe for little girls like her. Her mind was made up.

Sonia was a regular viewer of the television legal drama *Perry Mason*. She credits the show with her interest in the law.

Diabetes

US Supreme Court Justice Sonia Sotomayor has suffered from type I diabetes since she was a child. Only about 15 percent of people suffering with diabetes are diagnosed with type I diabetes and only 5 percent of the general population has it. But exactly what is it?

Basically, the body has stopped producing insulin. The body normally produces insulin to help the body turn sugar, starch, and the food we eat into energy. No one really knows what causes type 1 diabetes and it is treated mainly by daily insulin injections. Without the insulin, the disease is fatal. It is also very important for those suffering from type 1 diabetes to carefully monitor the foods they eat, especially the carbohydrates that are later turned into sugar by the body.

There are ways to prevent the more common type 2 diabetes, mainly with diet and exercise.

But as fate would have it, during a routine visit to the doctor to treat her serious diabetes, Sonia learned what kinds of jobs people with diabetes could do. But she also learned for the first time that there were several professions people with diabetes could never do. They included things like airline pilot and bus driver. But further on down the list she saw the words "police officer." Her dream of being the real-life Nancy Drew was crushed.

But maybe there was something better. Sonia had always thought that Nancy Drew's father was great in the books and he was a lawyer. And it just so happened that her and Junior's favorite television show every week was *Perry Mason*, a show about a lawyer who worked hard every episode to get to the truth behind every case.

Sonia became fascinated with the legal system. She loved watching the interaction between the defense attorney and the prosecutor. She loved these new words she was learning every week that they used in the courtroom. But, with every passing episode, she found that more and more her eye was drawn to the person in charge of the courtroom who rules over things wearing black robes—the judge.

Academics were an area in which Sotomayor thrived. She would become adjunct professor at New York University's School of Law.

Chapter 5

COMPUTER HEAD

Sonia continued her studies, earning the nickname "Computer-head," because she knew so much. She studied hard because she was determined to live out her dream and become a lawyer. She knew, from watching just about every law drama on television, that lawyers needed to be great speakers. They had the power to persuade a jury, convince a judge, and trick a prosecutor into admitting something they were trying to conceal. They needed to be believable, trustworthy, and most of all had to be great speakers. That was a problem.

Facing Her Fears to Improve Herself

While Sonia had no trouble expressing herself to her mother, her friends, and especially her little brother whenever he got on her nerves—which was more often than not—she had trouble speaking in public. She never felt very comfortable speaking in front of her class. She couldn't imagine having to speak in front of a crowded courtroom filled with people eagerly listening to every single word she said.

So, if she was ever going to be a lawyer, she would have to overcome that fear. She signed up to be one of the readers at church on Sundays. This was a person who would stand before the congregation and read a preselected bible passage that the priest would later talk about during his homily.

She nearly passed out from fright and nerves the very first time she rose from her seat and approached the pulpit to read. Somehow she would have to get past this fear. But even though her voice cracked and her forehead was sweating, she somehow got through the reading. And each week it became easier to do. Soon, Sonia had no trouble speaking in public.

New School and New Home

By the time she graduated from Blessed Sacrament after completing the eighth grade, Sonia decided to continue her Catholic school education by attending Cardinal Spellman High School. When Sonia attended the school, the boys and girls were kept separated in different parts of the school. They were allowed to mingle during lunch and certain advanced classes.

During summer vacation between her freshman and sophomore years, Sonia landed her first job, working in a ladies clothing store. But things were getting dangerous in her neighborhood and the once-safe Bronxdale Houses were now a haven for drugs and violence. Her mother started looking at places to move and she moved

Sonia graduated the eighth grade from Blessed Sacrament and began high school at Cardinal Spellman.

her family to a new apartment complex in the very northeast corner of the Bronx called Co-op City. The apartments were brand new and spacious and there were people of every color and ethnic background moving in. The Sotomayors' apartment also was very close to Cardinal Spellman High School. For the first time in her life, Sonia was able to have her own bedroom.

Her high school years world represent a lot of firsts. It was the first time she started to learn analytically instead of just memorizing facts and it was the first time she started to go on dates with boys. And, of course, the first time she fell in love.

His name was Kevin Noonan and Sonia and he were practically inseparable throughout high school. They did everything together and he started spending lots of time in Co-op City with Sonia and her family. Maybe it was a silly thought, but Sonia had a feeling she would one day marry her high school sweetheart.

As she progressed through high school, Sonia joined the school's debate team and surprised even herself with how well she was able to come up with convincing arguments to topics that were just given to her. She even won a few competitions. And with each debate that she won she became more and more confident.

Pretty soon it was junior year and time to start applying for colleges. She never really thought about what schools she would be applying to but a close friend and classmate, who was a few years older, was attending

Co-op City

Co-op City, where Sonia Sotomayor spent her teenage years, is a huge apartment complex built in the Northeast Bronx. It was constructed in a swampy area that used to be home to an amusement park known as "Freedomland," that was a popular attraction in the early 1960s. It is so big in fact, that it is regarded as the largest cooperative housing complex in the world. And, if it were really its own city, it would be the 10th biggest city in New York State.

Construction started in the mid-1960s and the first residents started moving in by 1968. Co-op City has its own power plant, which generates electricity to all 35 hi-rise buildings, its own security force, and its own educational park that features a high school, two elementary schools, and two intermediate or junior high schools.

The new buildings, parks and shopping plazas made the area attractive for many Bronx residents who were looking to move out of housing projects or slums. For many years it was known as a beautiful place to live. But shoddy construction work and corrupt deals during the building phase caused many problems years later and there were numerous legal battles and even a rent-strike as residents demanded improvements and repairs.

Besides Sonia Sotomayor, Co-op City's most famous former resident is rapper and actress Queen Latifah, who lived there in the 1980s.

The demographics of Co-op City have changed over the years. When it first opened, the majority of people who lived there were Jewish American, Irish American, and Italian American. By 2014, 80 percent of the population is reported to be African American or Hispanic. Today Co-op City is home to nearly 45,000 residents.

The Sotomayors moved to Co-op City, a large new complex in the Bronx.

Princeton University. This was and remains an elite school in the Ivy League.

Up until this point, Sonia's entire world had been the Bronx and Puerto Rico. She didn't know anything about the Ivy League or how tough it was to get into these schools. But her friend urged her to apply to these schools, telling her she was smart enough.

Princeton

She did and was accepted into several prestigious Ivy League schools. After visiting a few of them, she decided to attend Princeton, which is located in New Jersey. Her mother could not have been prouder as all the doctors

The Ivy League

Sonia Sotomayor was fortunate and hard-working enough to attend and graduate from two Ivy League schools. The Ivy League is made up of eight institutions of higher learning. They are Yale University, Harvard University, Princeton University, Cornell University, Columbia University, Dartmouth College, Brown University, and the University of Pennsylvania.

Ivy League schools are known as being among the top in the nation academically and remain very difficult or competitive to gain admittance as a student. The schools are also known as being among the world leaders in conducting research and publishing the results.

All eight schools have expansive histories as they have been around for a very long time. The oldest, Harvard, opened in 1636. The newest, Cornell, opened its doors in 1865.

The term Ivy League was started by sports writers because it became a tradition among graduating seniors at the respective schools to plant ivy along the outer walls of the school's buildings. The Ivy League became a collegiate athletic conference where teams from the schools played each other. They remain athletic rivals with each other but typically are no longer considered powerhouse football or basketball teams as they once were.

and nurses where she worked made such a big deal about Sonia going to such a special school.

This was when Sonia realized just how small her life experience had been to that point. She started meeting people from all over the country and all over the world. Most of them had come from expensive preparatory schools and lives that included traveling, culture, museums, and art galleries. It caused Sonia to retreat a little bit in her own mind. She was not the same confident student she was at Cardinal Spellman or even at Blessed Sacrament.

Doubt started to creep in and Sonia wondered if she even belonged at a school like Princeton. There were

Sotomayor had doubts that she belonged at an Ivy League school like Princeton.

things like computers that she had to learn about and she had never read any of the classic books that her new classmates spoke about. She had never even heard about the classic story *Alice in Wonderland*!

Needless to say, Sonia started spending lots of time in the library trying to make up for lost time. She knew that she would never have the same background or lifestyle of many of her wealthy classmates but she refused to get left behind in the classroom. Still, the lack of experience and worldliness made her one of the quietest students around. She barely raised her hand to even answer a question her entire freshman year, out of fear of sounding dumb.

The weekends were better. Her high school boyfriend, Kevin, would drive from his college in New York every Friday night and spend the entire weekend by Sonia's side. Most of the time was spent studying and trying not to fall too far behind.

Things got rough and a part of Sonia was crushed when her grandmother became ill with cancer and died soon after. She finally understood her mother's depression when Sonia's father had died. Things were different. Who knew life was going to be this hard?

Getting Involved in Politics

Luckily, she made a friend on campus who had a similar background. Her new friend was a Puerto Rican girl from New York as well. But she was confident and outspoken. Sonia wanted to be like her. The girl urged Sonia to join a Puerto Rican activist group for women called *Accion Puertoriquena.* The group was welcoming to other Puerto Rican students so they would not feel so alone upon first coming to Princeton.

And, like many other student groups, they started getting active in politics and would protest things like the ongoing Vietnam War. One of the big issues the group faced was trying to convince the college to hire more qualified Puerto Ricans, especially in high positions like professors. Sonia was never comfortable holding signs or yelling slogans. Her strength was in debate, so she started regularly writing letters and articles for the school newspaper.

Lasting change normally happens slowly and slowly Sonia was making a difference. Her letters were getting printed. Her voice was being heard. She was even behind efforts that resulted in Princeton offering a course in Puerto Rican history. She joined other committees as well, like the Discipline Committee and the Third World Center. She enjoyed being a voice for justice. It would be her voice for years to come.

Chapter 6

From Princeton to Yale

o say Sotomayor's Princeton experience was a success would be a wild understatement. She not only was awarded the Moses Taylor Pyne Honor Prize—the highest award any graduating senior can receive, but she was also accepted into the Phi Beta Kappa Society, reserved for only the brightest and best students. She would be graduating with the highest honors; not too shabby for a girl who had not even heard of *Alice in Wonderland* just a few years earlier. Sonia had her future mapped out and she was determined to follow it.

Law School and Marriage

First on the list was getting into a law school. Her accomplishments at Princeton made it possible for her to get into just about any law school she wanted. Again, she chose the Ivy League and was accepted to Yale Law

While at law school at Yale, Sotomayor made important contacts who would be instrumental to her career.

School in New Haven, Connecticut. The second on her list was getting married to her longtime sweetheart before she was too old. Kevin Noonan had graduated from college as well and was thinking of either medical school, graduate school, or law school. Since he was undecided, it made sense that he move with Sotomayor to Yale.

The happy couple got married that summer after Sonia graduated from Princeton. They got married in a small chapel and celebrated at a Queens catering hall. Everyone was happy and the newlywed couple would soon be moving to New Haven to begin the next adventure in their lives.

All those years after being fascinated by television courtroom dramas and especially with fictional lawyer Perry Mason, Sotomayor was enrolled in one of the best law schools in the entire nation and about to make her dreams come true.

And while it took her a while to fit in on the campus and college life at Princeton, she had no such troubles at Yale. In fact, one of the first people she met would become a mentor to her and help guide her along the amazing career she was starting.

Jose Cabranes, Mentor

While Sotomayor always enjoyed good relationships with her teachers and older, more experienced students, she always wanted to be friends with someone who had truly made a difference as a lawyer. Maybe it was the

Perry Mason

So exactly just who was this fictional television lawyer that once inspired a future US Supreme Court Justice?

Well, before noted television actor Raymond Burr made the character a household name in the 1960s, Perry Mason lived solving cases and protecting the innocent on the pages of more than 80 novels and short stories written by crime fiction writer Erle Stanley Gardner.

Gardner's creation was a lawyer who loved challenges. Perry Mason would often take on clients and cases that seemed impossible to win or who seemed guilty beyond a reasonable doubt. The character, who was also immortalized on a long-running radio show before television, liked the challenge.

In the mid-1930s, Hollywood produced several films featuring the character Perry Mason. He would normally successfully defend his client by investigating the crime himself and finding the guilty party, who usually confessed when faced with the facts. It is interesting that despite being featured in so many stories and novels, radio shows, films and television programs, Gardner never really wrote a lot about Mason's private life. The public really only ever got to know Perry Mason the hotshot lawyer.

The format for the television series that captured the imagination of a little girl in a cramped Bronx apartment was always the same. The first 30 minutes of the hour-long show dealt with the crime and the motives numerous people had for committing it. The second 30 minutes always took place inside the courtroom.

influence of her grandmother, but Sotomayor always recognized the value of learning from her elders.

At Yale she was introduced to a lawyer by the name of Jose Cabranes, who was a special advisor to the governor of Puerto Rico as well as serving as the lawyer for the Yale Law School.

The pair hit it off immediately and Sotomayor was fascinated by the work her new friend did. She was especially interested in research he was conducting regarding the citizenship of Puerto Ricans born on and still living on the Caribbean island. The question in his research centered on the future citizenship of all those people should Puerto Rico one day become an independent nation.

It was clear from the start that Sotomayor admired Cabranes deeply. "He was a trailblazer and a hero to many for his work promoting civil rights for Hispanics," Sotomayor wrote in her book.[1] He taught her the importance of looking at a topic objectively and without emotion. This was not something Sonia was initially able to do regarding her feelings about the island where her parents were born. But it was something she learned quickly and a lesson that would stay with her through her entire law career all the way up to the United States Supreme Court.

She started assisting him in his research and at the same time another very important door opened for her. In medical school and law school it is very important and prestigious to get "published." Students often do in-depth research papers with the goals of having them appear in one important and respected journal or another. In Sotomayor's case, just about every law student at Yale wanted to one day be published in the *Yale Law Journal*. She came up with an idea for a paper while assisting Cabranes, and the journal published her paper on Puerto Rico and statehood.

Mock Trials

One of the things Sonia loved most about law school were the mock trials. This was when she and her classmates would set up a criminal case and try to prosecute it. They often brought in a jury of people from the neighborhood, who were paid to participate in these valuable training exercises.

From the very start she remembered the Perry Mason character from television and the fearless way he seemed to attack the evidence. And even though she might have been nervous at times, she never let it show.

It was during these exercises that she learned to read people's faces, something any successful lawyer must learn to do. She would watch the jury intently as she spoke. Was her argument too simple? Was it too complicated? Was the jury paying attention or was she boring them? Was she behaving too aggressively or did she need to step up her game? The law school students were allowed to speak with and question the people brought in to play the jury for these mock trials after they were all done. Sonia made it a point to quiz as many as she could to gather as much information about how

Sotomayor thrived at law school, developing valuable skills and gaining confidence in herself.

jurors saw her as she could. She viewed every minute, every assignment, and every training exercise as an opportunity to learn and get better.

She didn't just want to be a lawyer. She wanted to be the best.

Not all law deals with criminal cases and arguing like Perry Mason though. And one summer, while she was studying at Yale, Sonia landed a temporary job at a big New York City law firm where she gained valuable experience in corporate law that involved things like contracts and antitrust lawsuits. The work was hard and when the job ended she realized she would have to work even harder if she wanted to be a well-rounded attorney that was well-versed in all types of law.

Public Defender Sotomayor

Like her time at Princeton, Sonia started getting involved in several groups and again, writing and editing were once again passionate topics for her. She worked her way up to the very prestigious position of editor of the *Yale Law Journal*, she also became the managing editor of a student-run publication on campus. This work— reading, editing, and writing about previous cases and case law history—would set her up for her first job as an attorney when she graduated from Yale with her law degree.

But exactly what kind of law would she be practicing? Well, as fate would have it, Sonia attended a conference/ job fair on campus that featured keynote speaker New York City District Attorney Robert Morgenthau. He said

New York City District Attorney Robert Morgenthau hired Sotomayor for her first legal job out of Yale.

Robert Morgenthau

Robert Morgenthau might just be the most well-known district attorney of our time. Yes, he is more than the person who gave Sonia Sotomayor her first job as a lawyer. Born into a very influential and political family in New York City in 1919, Morgenthau served in the US armed forces during World War II before starting his career as a prosecutor. His father had been the US Secretary of the Treasury and his grandfather was a US ambassador during World War I.

Morgenthau was named a federal prosecutor by President John F. Kennedy and stayed in that position for many years. He resigned to run for governor of New York State but lost. It was his work as the district attorney—or prosecutor—in New York City's borough of Manhattan that earned him the most fame. Morgenthau took over the post in 1975 and held it until his retirement in 2009. He was elected to the position eight times! That makes him the second-longest tenured district attorney in American history.

The Yale Law School graduate was known for being very tough on crime in the streets as well as what is known as "white-collar crime," that usually had to do with banking, stocks, and fraud. He was also known as the man who prosecuted Mark David Chapman, who killed famous musician John Lennon of the Beatles.

something that caused Sonia to perk up immediately. He said there are hundreds of assistant district attorneys in his office who tried criminal cases in front of juries and judges on their very first year on the job.

Patience was never one of Sonia's strong points and when she heard this she knew that was the job for her. She immediately spoke to Morgenthau—who was good friends with Cabranes—and before long she was offered a job. This was a shock to many of her classmates. Assistant district attorneys as well as public defenders, do not make a lot of money and someone with a law degree from Yale Law School typically goes to work for a big law firm where they get paid lots and lots of money.

But for Sotomayor, law has never been about trying to get rich. Perhaps it is because she grew up in poverty or maybe it is because she despised all forms of prejudice and the unfair way so many minorities and poor had been treated over the years. No, for Sonia Sotomayor it was never about the money, it has always been about the pursuit of justice.

When Sotomayor began working in the District Attorney's office, crime in New York City was at a high level.

Chapter 7

PUTTING THE BAD GUYS AWAY

Maybe it was a case of being in the right place at the right time. But when Sotomayor became a bright-eyed assistant district attorney in New York City in 1979 she couldn't have picked a better time to start—that is, of course, if she liked action.

New York City, like many major cities, was going through one of its rough patches and crime was at an all-time high. For Sotomayor, being a prosecutor at this time might have resembled trying to put bad guys in jail during the outlaw days of the Wild West.

Crime was rampant. It is no accident that this was about the same time that the drug cocaine started to become very popular in New York, followed by the even more addictive drug, crack. This spawned a new, dangerous type of drug addict that was more violent and more desperate to steal money for drugs. Purses were getting snatched. Chains and other jewelry were being ripped right off of people's necks. There was nowhere in the big city that seemed safe. The drugs had turned everything upside down. Things were so hectic and so busy in the police stations, jails, and courthouses that new assistant district attorneys were handling everything from misdemeanors, or minor crimes to murder cases.

During her time at Yale Law School, Sotomayor earned the reputation of "arguing like a man." At first, she was offended by the sexist comment, but then she began to understand that—though misguided—it meant she never backed down or allowed herself to get intimidated.

It was that bulldog mentality and attitude that helped her survive during those first few years as a prosecutor in New York. And that earned her high praise from her new boss. "Some of the judges like to push around young assistants and get them to dispose of cases," Morgenthau told the *New York Times*. "Well, no one pushed around Sonia Sotomayor; she stood up to the judges in an appropriate way."[1]

In truth, Sotomayor was terrific at the job, like she had been at just about everything else she put her mind to. She had no problem at all being in the limelight and working high-profile cases or prosecuting people who had committed very serious crimes.

Challenges at the DA's Office

However, she did have a problem with the some of the minor crimes. She did not like to see poor people get punished for petty crimes that they never would have

Sotomayor was a perfect fit for the DA's office. She was smart, assertive, and liked to be challenged.

SONIA SOTOMAYOR: FIRST LATINA SUPREME COURT JUSTICE

committed had they not lived in poverty. "I had more problems during my first year in the office with the low-grade crimes—the shoplifting, the prostitution, the minor assault cases," she told the *New York Times*. "In large measure, in those cases you were dealing with socioeconomic crimes, crimes that could be the product of the environment and of poverty. Once I started doing felonies it became less hard. …I'm still outraged by crimes of violence."[2] She was also saddened to see crimes committed by Hispanics on other Hispanics, often saying that the saddest crimes were the ones her "own people commit against each other."

Even though these things saddened her, she still did her job and prosecuted even the smallest misdemeanors with the same fire and energy as if she were prosecuting a high-profile murder. She would later admit that this was only because she was so nervous about making a mistake. She wanted to be the most prepared attorney in the courtroom no matter how serious the charge.

But, like her childhood hero Perry Mason, she wanted the truth to come out even if that meant she wouldn't win a case. In her book, *My Beloved World*, she recounts the story of a young man who was arrested for snatching a purse. The evidence was weak, the witness could not identify the man, and the purse was never found. The man declared his innocence and it seemed as if he was just in the wrong place at the wrong time when the police saw him. Sotomayor expressed her concern about the case to her boss, who urged her to prosecute it anyway.

Felonies vs. Misdemeanors

What's the difference between a felony and a misdemeanor? The simple answer is that misdemeanor crimes or offenses are not as serious as felony crimes or offenses. But, in general, every state in the United States has its own guidelines and laws regarding what is a felony and what is a misdemeanor.

The states generally separate the two categories based on punishment during sentencing. The standard is one year. So, if the punishment for being found guilty of a specific crime is more than one year in prison, then it is likely considered a felony. Anything that carries a sentence of less than one year in prison is normally a misdemeanor.

For example, murder would be considered a felony while shoplifting a small item would most likely be a misdemeanor. In some states there are charges known as "wobblers," meaning the prosecutor has the option of charging that crime as a felony or as a misdemeanor.

There are other offenses that can cause people to get in trouble with the law that are not as serious as a misdemeanor or a felony, and those are called infractions. Sometimes they are called petty crimes or violations. These typically include traffic or driving violations and other minor offenses.

She refused and said she would rather quit her job than lie to a jury and say that this man was guilty.

Having grown up in the projects and tough neighborhoods gave Sotomayor somewhat of an edge over many of her peers. She was as comfortable in the rough neighborhoods of the South Bronx or Harlem as she was on an Ivy League campus. So she was never afraid to go to these high-crime neighborhoods to seek out and interview witnesses that might help her convict a criminal.

She learned right away that juries react more to emotion and a sense of right and wrong than they do to the facts in the case. After she lost two trials in a row, she realized that she needed to be more convincing to the jury and tell them it was their right and obligation to find the person guilty if the evidence supported that. She remembered the work she did at Yale with the mock trials and tried to read the jurors and their emotions better. She never had a problem again.

She became very successful and soon earned a reputation, even among some of the more harsh judges, as being a lawyer who was fair and always prepared to try her cases. It seemed Sotomayor was a rising star. "If you can handle a felony case load in New York County, you can run a small country," Warren Murray, one of Sotomayor's bosses in the felony division, told CNN.[3]

Major Life Changes

The problem with working only in criminal law is that the overwhelming majority of people you ever deal with

Being raised in the Bronx helped Sotomayor do her job well. She was not afraid to visit rough neighborhoods to interview witnesses.

The Tarzan Burglar

Sotomayor credits one particularly tough case with helping her really learn the ropes of her job and what it took to be successful. It was known as the "Tarzan case." Tarzan is a fictional character raised by apes in the jungles of Africa from a baby after his family is killed. He would learn to move like his ape family, travelling by swinging from tree to tree hanging on to long vines.

In this case, Robert Maddicks was on trial known as the "Tarzan burglar." He would swing from building to building using a series of ropes and cables. He would burglarize top floor apartments, shooting anyone in his way. For a long time the police could not figure out how these apartments were being robbed.

It was big news in all of the newspapers and the public watched the trial closely to see if Maddicks would be convicted. The trial lasted five weeks as Sotomayor tied together all the evidence and witnesses in order to convince the jury that Maddicks was guilty. During the trial she questioned more than 20 witnesses on the stand. The jury even cried as Sotomayor questioned the sister of a man that Maddicks shot and killed.

In a key move, Sonia was able to convince Maddicks's girlfriend to testify against him in exchange for a reduced sentence on a different crime she had been convicted of. It all paid off as Maddicks was convicted and sentenced to more than 60 years in prison.

are those who have been accused of committing a crime. It can be very tiring and after a while you can forget that not everyone is a criminal. With that in mind, Sonia began volunteering for the Puerto Rican Legal Defense and Education Fund, working on legal matters that concerned Puerto Rican concerns.

She loved the important work even though it added to her already long days. She was routinely working 15 hours a day for the district attorney's office. This was starting to put a strain on her marriage to Noonan.

Without realizing it, they had grown apart. He had continued his studies and would become a patent lawyer and Sonia was usually too wrapped up at night in her caseload that the two barely spoke. It wasn't until they went away together on a much-needed vacation that they realized they no longer had anything to talk about.

They decided to split up. Sotomayor moved back to Co-op City into her mother's apartment, while Noonan stayed in New Jersey where they lived. They saw each other on and off for the next year, hoping an occasional date might re-spark their once strong love. But it did not work. They stayed friends and continued to be supportive of each other, but the passionate love was definitely gone. In 1983 the high school sweethearts divorced.

It was to be a time of new beginnings and change for everyone involved. Sotomayor decided she had enough of putting bad people in prison for a while and decided to leave the District Attorney's Office. No one was surprised. Unless one plans on staying a prosecutor their entire life, most people only do it for a few years before moving on to something else.

For Sonia, the turning point was prosecuting the same people over and over again for the same crimes. They would go to prison, get released, and then commit the same crime again. It was like banging her head against the wall. She started to doubt the importance of her work and wondered if maybe there was a better way to make the criminal justice system.

She remembered her old dream, the one started watching Perry Mason on television, and wondered if this was the right time to start following it. Maybe the time had come to start working on one day becoming a judge.

Chapter 8

Sotomayor knew that to be a judge, she would have to vary her experience as a lawyer. After all, judges have to preside over all types of cases including divorces, tax disputes, small claims, contracts, civil rights, lawsuits, and many other civil matters.

She decided to leave the criminal arena for a while and work as a civil law attorney. It was time to broaden her experience. "To be a judge I would need to learn to move comfortably in that world," she wrote in her book, *My Beloved World*. "And so I decided that my next job would be an immersion in civil law."[1]

Morgenthau knew how valuable Sonia was and tried talking her out of leaving. He talked about making her a bureau chief; that kind of position could lead to a state judge position. He even started giving her very challenging and high-profile cases to keep her happy. But her mind was made up.

After five years at the district attorney's office, Sotomayor moved on to work at Parvia & Harcourt.

Parvia & Harcourt

She went looking for a firm where she could make a difference. And she knew exactly what she wanted as well. She did not want to be one of those research lawyers who never sets foot in court but instead prepares documents. She loved the action and limelight of being in court. She found just the right firm: Parvia & Harcourt.

The firm had fancy offices and about thirty attorneys working for them. Those five years as a prosecutor, tirelessly working one case after another, had prepared Sotomayor to work just about anywhere. Remember, her former boss, Warren Murray, said she was now qualified to run a small country. She excelled in civil law, outworking and outmaneuvering her colleagues and peers. She did, however, have to buy a new wardrobe. She was expected to look the part of a highly-paid attorney instead of a gritty prosecutor. In one case, she was representing a famous handbag designer, Fendi, against counterfeiters. These are people who made bags that looked like real Fendi bags but weren't and sold them on the streets of Manhattan and in small retail shops. With the help of a private investigator, Sonia brought down the illegal gang that was making the bags. She even chased down some of the culprits who tried to flee while on the back of a motorcycle. The gang was very angry and they threatened her life. For a while she had to travel with police protection, something she never needed during all of her years as a prosecutor sending people to prison.

That case helped convince her bosses to make her a partner in the firm after only four years. She also developed close ties with the Fendi family and attended many fancy parties stocked with celebrities as their guest. In her book, *My Beloved World*, Sotomayor recalled an incredible and telling conversation with the owners of Parvia & Harcourt the night they made her a partner. "It's clear that you won't stay in private practice forever," George Parvia told her. "We know you're destined for the bench (judge) someday. Dave [Harcourt] is even convinced that you will go all the way to the Supreme Court."[2] They asked her to stay with the firm until she became a judge and she agreed. How could they possibly know this girl from the Bronx would one day wear the black robes on the US Supreme Court bench?

Trying New Things

During this time period, Sotomayor experienced a confidence spurt that allowed her to sign up for dancing lessons so she could finally learn how to *salsa* as well as learn many other popular dances. She was also able to finally conquer a lifelong apprehension of the water and learned how to swim. Sonia also started teaching law courses at New York University and Columbia University. She made lots of friends during this period and spent time socializing and sharing a summer home with friends in a place called Fire Island. She even started seeing a specialist to help control her diabetes.

Everything was clicking both personally and professionally. It seemed as if her dream was closer than

The governor of New York at the time, Mario Cuomo, appointed
Sotomayor to the state's mortgage agency in 1987.

ever. And soon, more valuable experience arrived. In 1987 the governor of New York, Mario Cuomo, appointed Sotomayor to the board of the state's mortgage agency, where she would volunteer her time to defend the rights of the poor when it came to matters of housing.

Mario Cuomo

Governor Mario Cuomo was one of the most well-known politicians of his time. He was so popular within the Democratic Party and was such a powerful speaker in fact, that many people urged him to run for the presidency of the United States on more than one occasion. He always declined and instead spent nearly his entire life serving the people of New York. He served as the fifty-second governor of New York from 1983 to 1994. Before that he spent three years as Lieutenant Governor and another three as the Secretary of State for New York.

Cuomo was born in Queens, New York and attended St. John's University, where he earned his degree and was drafted as a standout baseball player by the Pittsburgh Pirates. His playing career came to an end when he suffered an injury after being hit in the head with a baseball. Returning to St. John's for his law degree, he practiced law for several years before deciding to enter the world of politics. Cuomo ran unsuccessfully for Mayor of New York before eventually being elected governor of the state. He retired from politics in 1994 and died on New Year's Day, 2015, of natural causes. His son Andrew was elected governor of New York in 2010, carrying the Cuomo name further into the history books of New York politics. Another son, Chris, is a journalist for the Cable News Network, CNN.

Federal District Judge

Her work on the board did not go unnoticed and only four years later, in 1991, the President of the United States, George H. W. Bush nominated Sotomayor to be a federal district judge in the Southern District of New York. The nomination was supported by a state senator from New York named Patrick Moynihan, who like Sotomayor had grown up in poverty and attended Catholic schools growing up before making a name for himself as one of New York's leaders. Moynihan also knew that it was time the state had a Hispanic federal judge to reflect the large Hispanic population in New York.

After about 18 months of background checks and confirming the nomination, Sonia Sotomayor was sworn in as a judge in 1992, becoming the first-ever Hispanic federal judge in the state. It was an historic occasion. The ceremony lasted only five minutes, but for Sotomayor it seemed to happen in perfect slow motion.

For Sotomayor, it was all very emotional. She savored the feeling of the soft black robes and the oath that she took promising to judge impartially regardless of religion or social background or whether the participants in court were poor or rich. She celebrated with her mother, who after all those years of being a lonely widow, had found a new boyfriend. That made the occasion even happier for Sotomayor.

In a funny exchange, Sonia remembers how her mother didn't quite understand why she would want to leave the law firm where she was making a lot of money

Federal Court

Our government is broken up into three separate sections called "branches." They are the executive branch, which is the presidency, the legislative branch, which are the lawmakers in Congress and the judiciary, which are the courts. Congress decides how many federal judges there will be and what types of cases will be heard in federal court rather than a state or county court. Under the constitution however, it is the president who appoints federal judges.

There are three levels of federal court. The highest level is the US Supreme Court, also known as the "court of last resort." Below the US Supreme Court is the US Court of Appeals. The function of the appeals courts are to hear appeals based on rulings made in lower courts. An appeal is made when someone does not agree with a judge's decision or feels a new trial should be ordered because of certain reasons.

Below the US Court of Appeals are the US District Courts. There are only 94 of them in the country and that was the type of court that President George H.W. Bush appointed Sotomayor to. Both civil and criminal cases are heard in this court. Every state has at least one federal district court. These are the highest courts where trials still take place. The other two branches of federal court merely listen to appeals and make judgments based on the evidence.

to become a judge making less money. In any event, because she was representing the Southern District, which included the Bronx, she would have to live there. So she left Brooklyn and moved closer to her mother.

Her experience practicing all types of law had prepared her for the position. She heard cases involving fraud and white collar crime to lawsuits filed by prison inmates wanting more religious freedoms.

Sotomayor's first month as a judge was terrifying. She was unsure of herself and doubted her every move. She moved through her calendar slowly and carefully so as to not make any embarrassing mistakes. She even admits to being so nervous during her first trial—one that involved the notorious motorcycle gang the "Hell's Angels"—that she could hear her knees knocking together from under her desk. Even today, Justice Sotomayor falls into bouts of self-doubt. It can probably be traced back to those early years at Princeton where she felt inferior to some of her rich, well-educated classmates.

"I have spent my years since Princeton, while at law school and in my various professional jobs, not feeling completely a part of the worlds I inhabit," she told the *New York Times* in 2009. "I am always looking over my shoulder wondering if I measure up."[3] Maybe it is those occasional moments of doubt that force her to work harder than anyone else. Maybe that is one of the reasons for her success. She did measure up and had to preside and rule over some very high-profile cases, including one where she ruled it unconstitutional for the

Her years of practicing law as an attorney prepared Sotomayor for her next step: federal district judge.

city of White Plains to ban a Jewish religious symbol, the menorah, from being displayed in a public park.

But it was one case in particular that would put Sonia Sotomayor on the public stage and earn her many supporters. It was a case that earned her the nickname— for a while anyway—the "savior of baseball."

A passionate baseball fan, Sotomayor was particularly interested in taking on the baseball strike.

Chapter 9

A FEDERAL ISSUE

otomayor's love of baseball goes all the way back to her early childhood. Some of the fondest memories she has of her father are of him at her grandmother's house watching the New York Yankees on her small television. Those were the days before alcohol caused him to be angry and unpredictable. During those days, the Yankees were the only team in New York. The Dodgers and Giants had left the city in the 1950s for California and the Mets did not come into existence until 1962. Plus, Sonia's family lived in the South Bronx, within walking distance of Yankee Stadium, where the team plays its home games.

Like her father, the future Supreme Court Justice became a fan of the Yankees as well. She remembers watching them play in the World Series while she was studying law at Yale. Despite her busy schedule, Sotomayor always found the time to check on her favorite team to see how they were doing.

Sotomayor Saves Baseball

Little did she know that her position as a Federal Court judge would be able to positively affect the sport she's always loved. The union representing the Major League baseball players and the lawyers representing the owners were unable to come to a contract agreement in 1994. The owners threatened the players that they would eliminate their freedom to switch teams when their contracts were finished (free agency) as well as other problems.

The rising tensions between the two sides resulted in the worst possible thing for both sides and the worst possible thing for a baseball fan—the players went on strike. This meant they walked off the field and refused to play. The last month of the 1994 season, as well as the playoffs and World Series were cancelled. This was the first time ever that the World Series was not played! The strike lingered for more than two hundred days and was now threatening to cancel the 1995 season as well.

Baseball fans everywhere were nervous about the future of the game. "It was terrible," Paul Finkelman, an expert in sports law at Albany Law School told National Public Radio (NPR). "It almost destroyed baseball. If you are a baseball fan, a summer without baseball is a year without a summer."[1]

Indeed, all eyes would be watching. Baseball had already lost a lot of its popularity to football and basketball. An entire season being cancelled would just about kill the sport. That is when the case landed before Federal Courts Judge Sonia Sotomayor.

Baseball Work Stoppages

Maybe Sonia Sotomayor really did save baseball. There have been no work stoppages or missed games since that 1994 player's strike that cancelled the last month of the season and the World Series. Before 1994, there had been seven other labor disputes in Major League Baseball. Only two of the other work stoppages resulted in real games being missed. The first was in 1972, when a dispute over pensions caused the cancellation of the first 13 days of the baseball season. In all, 86 games were cancelled.

In 1981, a 50-day work stoppage over the issue of free agent compensation caused the cancellation of 712 games. When they resumed play, the season was split into two halves with the winner of each half qualifying for the playoffs. Other baseball work stoppages occurred in 1973, 1976, 1980, 1985, and 1990. A strike nearly took place in 2002 but owners and players agreed at the very last minute on a bargaining agreement and no games were missed. That contract lasted until 2006 and again no games were missed.

According to the court transcripts, Sotomayor told both sides that even though she was not familiar with the details of their dispute, she did know an awful lot about baseball. "You can't grow up in the South Bronx without knowing about baseball," she said in court, according to the transcripts.

It was March 30, 1995 and Sotomayor, who was only 40 at the time, would be asked to make her most important decision to date. She listened to both sides

Sotomayor's ruling ended the 1994 Major League Baseball strike just in time for the 1995 season.

complain about the other side and state their case. It did not take her long to come to her decision. In fact, it only took about fifteen minutes. While baseball fans were happy she made her decision so quickly, there were some who criticized her for being rash.

In the end she ruled in favor of the players and chastised the owners for not negotiating in good faith and trying to play by a new and different set of rules. In her ruling she also mentions how important the game and the issue is to the general public.

She ordered the owners to restore free agency and arbitration and to keep negotiating a new deal. With that, the players agreed to go back to work and the season was saved. "The owners misunderstood the case law, and many of their arguments were inconsistent," she said in her ruling. "One side can't come up with new rules unless they negotiate it with the other." The owners appealed her ruling but an appellate court agreed with her decision and the baseball strike was over.

Sotomayor started receiving praise from many people. "It was the correct ruling," said Rick Karcher, sports law professor at the Florida Coastal School of Law in a *Time* magazine article from 2009. "She assured that fair collective bargaining would take place under the labor laws."[2] President Barack Obama said that Sonia, "may have saved the game of baseball."

One of the other highlights of her tenure as a federal court judge was accomplished the very night she was sworn in. Sonia had the privilege of acting as the official when her mother decided to marry again. It was one of those special nights that she will never forget.

The Court of Appeals

Now, a few years later with such a high-profile case behind her, it was only a matter of time before she would move up and be appointed to the US Court of Appeals. After six solid years on the district court, Sotomayor received some good news. It came in the form of a phone call from Washington D.C. The message? President Bill Clinton had nominated her to fill a vacancy on the Court of Appeals for the Second Circuit. She was ecstatic. If appointed, she would be only one step from the highest court in the land.

During one of the questionnaires she had to fill out during the process, Sotomayor wrote: "Judges must be extraordinarily sensitive to the impact of their decisions and function within, and respectful of, the constitution."[3]

During the nomination process, Sonia experienced a true dream come true when she went on a tour of the White House. "It's hard to describe in words what that afternoon visit to the White House was like for me," she said during a speech at Pace University, which was honoring her with a special degree.

> I was overwhelmed. As some people in the audience may know, I grew up in a South Bronx housing project. I am the child of first generation immigrant Puerto Ricans to New York City. As I was growing up, none of my cousins in New York had yet graduated from college. I was, however, a child with dreams.

Private About Private Life

Sonia Sotomayor talks openly about her mother, father, and brother—now an allergy doctor in upstate New York. She also writes extensively about her early relationship with Kevin Noonan, her childhood sweetheart whom she married and later divorced. But other than that, she is fiercely private about her private life. She mentions in her book that she remained close friends with Noonan but that was really about it.

When she was going through the nomination process for the appellate court, she was photographed with a construction contractor named Peter White. He also helped her on with her robes when she was finally confirmed. Sonia introduced him as her fiancé. But the two broke up a short while after she was confirmed. She has never been romantically linked in public to anyone else and rarely talks about her personal life.

Later she would say that she is so inundated with work that she doesn't have time to date, but would like to one day when she feels she has time. She does spend time with some fellow justices and plays cards with them from time to time. She also admits to missing the days when no one really knew who she was and she could go dancing and take off her shoes and have fun without the risk of being photographed in the local newspaper.

I dreamed first of graduating from college. I was precocious enough to dream even of going to law school. I hoped to become a prosecutor and, I even imagined that someday, maybe, if life was really good to me, I would become a judge. The only kind of judge I knew about then was a criminal court judge because my only exposure to the law was from television. Back then, Perry Mason was the star TV attorney, and he only practiced criminal law. That afternoon six years ago in the White House, I realized I had lived my dreams and more incredibly, I had far surpassed them.[4]

The approval process took more than a year, which is not unusual as both Democrat and Republican lawmakers use their votes to try and swing deals with the other party. Her appointment was confirmed 67–29 in October 1998. She celebrated with her family.

She took the bench and this time it was much different than her appointment to the district court. There was no knee-knocking. She was not nervous at all. In fact she relished the appointment and the responsibility and quickly earned the reputation of being a no-nonsense type of judge. She hated when others were not prompt or were unprepared.

And throughout her years on the Appeals Court, she would always hold fast to the theme of justice, especially for the poor, that she carried with her from the very beginning. "We educated, privileged lawyers have a professional and moral duty to represent the underrepresented in our society, to ensure that justice

Like Sonia Sotomayor, Hillary Clinton was an ivy league-educated lawyer who turned to public service.

exists for all, both legal and economic justice," she told the *Hispanic Outlook in Higher Education* in 2002.[5]

Even if she was never elevated to the position of a US Supreme Court Justice, Sotomayor would have been very happy staying at the appellate level. She told a crowd of students and parents at Pace University just how lucky she was to be an appellate judge. "I love my work," she said. "It stimulates and challenges me. I wake up each morning excited about the prospect of engaging in work that fulfills me and gives me a chance to have a voice in the development of law."[6]

Chapter 10

SUPREMELY WONDERFUL

Sotomayor would remain on the appellate court for the better part of ten years, making very important rulings and decisions in numerous cases. Some of those cases were even appealed all the way up to the US Supreme Court. Over that 10-year span, Sotomayor would hear appeals in more than 3,000 cases and would write 380 majority opinions.

Staying True to Herself

Despite her ever-increasing role in the public light, Sotomayor always stayed humble and surrounded herself with very intelligent people whom she leaned on often. Many of her clerks and aides over the years have commended her for always wanting to know all sides of an issue before making any sort of ruling on it. In some cases, she would ask for printouts of entire court transcripts so she could read what was previously said during a trial.

One of Sotomayor's favorite pastimes is salsa dancing. She joined actor Esai Morales for a dance at the 13th Annual National Hispanic Foundation for the Arts Noche Musical in 2009.

She also developed the reputation of truly caring about the people she knows and their families. A New York lawyer, James Levine, who served as a clerk for Sotomayor in 2001 to 2002 said that she was the only one of the judges who interviewed him who cared to know anything about his family. In fact, he told the *New York Times* that her very first question was about his family. He would later say that it seemed she really wanted to get to know him as a person.

Other co-workers from this time period said she would often take them to watch the Yankees play at Yankee Stadium and sit in the bleachers with the rest of the fans who could not afford the better, more costly seats. She was often recognized and greeted loudly.

Other workers described her as energetic and hardworking. "Personality and style-wise she is a dynamo," former clerk Lisa Zornberg told the *New York Times*, ". . . who doesn't tolerate unpreparedness, nor should she."[1]

A free thinker, Sotomayor made two high-profile rulings that were unpopular and were later reversed by the same US Supreme Court she would later sit on. The first, a decision made in 2000, said that a man working for a government contractor was able to sue the company for violating his rights. Another ruling, made in 2007, favored environmental concerns over how much money a company would have to pay to abide by the strict rules.

It is clear, even though both decisions were reversed, Sotomayor continued to fight for the underdog and the less powerful. Even after her confirmation and appointment to the US Supreme Court, Sonia has stayed true to herself and to her ideals. She also is not afraid to let her personality show.

Supreme Court Justice

Sotomayor was sworn in to the United States Supreme Court on August 8, 2009. Being one of the youngest justices on the court did not deter her from distinguishing herself on the court and with her fellow justices. After serving one year on the Supreme Court, the justices held a party. But Sonia, who grew up with the raucous, all-night parties that featured dancing and poetry-reading at her grandmother's apartment was not going to be satisfied with the quiet, reserved get-together that had been arranged. Instead she had one of her staffers plug in some music and soon the salsa music began to play. One by one she urged all the other justices to stand up and dance. Needless to say, they were all pretty apprehensive but went up and danced with Sonia. "I knew she'd be trouble," Justice Antonin Scalia laughed after his turn to dance had finished, according to *Breaking In: The Rise of Sonia Sotomayor and the Politics of Justice* (2014) by Joan Biskupic.

But there was one justice who was certainly not in a dancing mood, not to mention she was in bad health: Justice Ruth Bader Ginsburg. Her husband, Marty, had died three days earlier and the elderly Ginsburg was still in a state of sorrow and mourning. Ginsburg told Sonia that she did not want to dance. But Sonia leaned in, according to the book by Biskupic, and whispered that

Sonia Sotomayor's 2013 memoir, *My Beloved World*, chronicles the Supreme Court justice's achievements and challenges.

Marty would have wanted her to dance. The pair danced for a few moment before Ginsburg put her hands gently on Sonia's face and thanked her.

Speaking for Those Who Have No Voice

Sotomayor remains an independent thinker not afraid to confront issues that make some people uncomfortable. This is evident in some of the rulings and opinions she has made during her tenure so far on the Supreme Court. In one such case, a 2013 affirmative action case called *Schuette v. BAMN,* Sotomayor made the argument in her dissenting opinion that despite the advancements, race still matters in this country. She basically rebuked fellow Chief Judge John Roberts, who once said the only way to stop discrimination is to stop discriminating.

This simplistic statement angered Sotomayor, who wanted it to be known that no one knows what it is like to be discriminated against unless they have actually experienced it. "[R]ace matters for reasons that really are only skin deep, that cannot be discussed any other way, and that cannot be wished away," she said.

> Race matters to a young man's view of society when he spends his teenage years watching others tense up as he passes, no matter the neighborhood where he grew up. Race matters to a young woman's sense of self when she states her hometown, and then is pressed, "No, where are you really from?" regardless of how many generations her family has been in the country. Race matters to a young person addressed by a stranger in a foreign language, which he does not understand because only English was spoken at home.

Women of the US Supreme Court

When Elena Kagan was appointed to the US Supreme Court in 2010, she became only the fourth woman to serve as a justice. Sotomayor was the third but who were the other two?

The first was Sandra Day O'Connor, who served 25 years after being appointed by President Ronald Reagan in 1981. She had previously served as a judge and then as an elected official in Arizona. She was confirmed by a vote of 99–0. One senator was absent and apologized to her later for not making the vote 100–0.

Ruth Bader Ginsburg, who followed O'Connor as the second female to serve on the highest court in the land, praised O'Connor for being a pioneer and for bringing a perspective that no one before had experienced.

"The first woman to serve on the Supreme Court brought to the Conference table experience others did not possess: the experience of growing up female in the 1930s, 40s, and 50s, of raising a family, of doing all manner of legal work— government service, private practice, successive successful candidacies for legislative and judicial office," Ginsburg would write in a tribute to O'Connor.[2]

Ginsburg was appointed in 1993 by President Bill Clinton, becoming the first Jewish female member of the Supreme Court.

Race matters because of the slights, the snickers, the silent judgments that reinforce that most crippling of thoughts: "I do not belong here."[3]

If it wasn't for Affirmative Action, Sotomayor and other people of different color and ethnic backgrounds would have never been admitted into schools like Princeton. She is not in favor of a quota system, meaning schools or employers must hire or admit a certain number of minorities, but instead they should look for candidates in places they had never looked before. She said it is perfectly normal to seek the comfort and strength from your own community and from those who look like you, but she urges everyone to use it as a "springboard to explore the larger world."

The Price Paid

While sitting as a justice on the highest court in the land was a longtime goal for Sotomayor, she admitted during an interview with television personality Oprah Winfrey that the position was a sacrifice and that the price she has paid is a certain level of happiness. Winfrey asked her point-blank if this is the most fun she has ever had. Sotomayor gave her a sad smile and then shook her head.

> No. I loved my life as a District Court and Circuit Court Judge. There, I could be more me. Nobody took pictures and nobody cared. I loved my work then. I had a freedom that when you become a justice, you're deprived of. That's not to suggest I'm unhappy, I have a wonderful life and I'm doing things I never imagined and I'm very, very grateful. . . . The life I gave up is the most fun I've ever had.[4]

Sotomayor always knew she wanted to serve the public and she knew that in doing so there would have to be certain sacrifices. Life may be harder as a Supreme Court Justice and there may be more pressures placed on

Oprah Winfrey

When Justice Sonia Sotomayor was interviewed by Oprah Winfrey on television, she followed a long line of famous faces who opened up about private matters to the woman so famous for her work on television that she can simply go by her first name. Oprah is a media mogul, actress, producer, and talk show host who rose to fame with the wildly popular *Oprah Winfrey Show*, which aired on television from 1986 to 2011.

Winfrey grew up dirt poor in rural Mississippi and suffered through many hardships as a child. But she followed her dreams and by the age of nineteen was a local television newswoman. She later moved to Chicago, where she became a daytime talk show host on a local station. Only a few months after getting started, her show was the highest-rated show in the area. This prompted the networks to offer her a syndicated deal, meaning her show would be shown all over the country instead of just Chicago.

What followed were awards, television specials, exclusive interviews, movie roles, and now she even owns her own network and she has never looked back. In 2015, a movie she produced and acted in—*Selma*—was nominated for the Academy Award for best picture.

Sotomayor has brought a certain vitality and a different perspective to the Supreme Court.

Although she holds one of the most important jobs in the country, Sotomayor is accessible and down to earth.

her, but she knows how important and valuable the work is, and the fact that she may be paving the way for other Hispanics and Hispanic women to make advancements where there were none before.

She draws strength from her community and actually promised President Obama that she would always stay connected to her roots, to the neighborhood and people of her childhood. "My community still today gives me strength," she said. "The kids I meet inspire me to keep going."[5] And she continues to inspire us with her incredible story.

Chronology

1954—Sonia Sotomayor is born in the Bronx on June 25.

1963—She is diagnosed with type I diabetes.

1963—Juan Sotomayor dies.

1976—Graduates from Princeton University.

1976—Marries high school sweetheart, Kevin Noonan.

1979—Graduates from Yale Law School.

1979 Starts work as a prosecutor in New York City.

1984—Leaves her job as prosecutor to enter the private sector. She starts working as an associate for the New York law firm Parvia & Harcourt and is later made a partner.

1992—After being nominated by President George H.W. Bush, Sotomayor is confirmed as a US District Judge for the Southern District of New York.

1995—Issues a ruling that essentially ends the baseball strike.

1998—Is nominated by President Bill Clinton for the US Circuit Court of Appeals for the Second Circuit.

2009—Is nominated by President Barack Obama for a vacant seat on the US Supreme Court.

Chapter Notes

CHAPTER 1. AMERICAN DREAM COME TRUE

1. "Remarks by the President in Nominating Judge Sonia Sotomayor to the United States Supreme Court," *The White House,* May 26, 2009, <http://www.whitehouse.gov/the_press_office/Remarks-by-the-President-in-Nominating-Judge-Sonia-Sotomayor-to-the-United-States-Supreme-Court>.

2. Keith B. Richburg, "Federal Judge Sonia Sotomayor Likely to Be on Obama's Shortlist," *Washington Post*, May 7, 2009.

3. Oprah Winfrey Network. "An Exciting Moment in Justice Sonia Sotomayor's Life: Oprah's Next Chapter: Oprah Winfrey Network," *YouTube,* March 25, 2013, <http://www.youtube.com/watch?v=9iUW84jPCHI>. Retrieved February, 2015.

4. "Remarks by the President."

5. Ibid.

6. Ibid.

7. Pace Law School Honorary Degree Acceptance Speech May 18, 2003.

CHAPTER 3. HUMBLE BEGINNINGS

1. Sheryl Gay Stolberg. "Sotomayor, a Trailblazer and a Dreamer," *New York Times,* May 26, 2009, <http://www.nytimes.com/2009/05/27/us/politics/27websotomayor.html?pagewanted=all&_r=0>.

2. Sonia Sotomayor, *My Beloved World* (New York: Knopf Publishing, 2013), p. 33.

CHAPTER 6. FROM PRINCETON TO YALE

1. Sonia Sotomayor. *My Beloved World* (New York: Knopf Publishing, 2013), p. 176.

CHAPTER 7. PUTTING THE BAD GUYS AWAY

1. Sheryl Gay Stolberg. "Sotomayor, a Trailblazer and a Dreamer," *New York Times,* May 26, 2009, <http://www.nytimes.com/2009/05/27/us/politics/27websotomayor.html?pagewanted=all&_r=0>.
2. Ibid.
3. Ann O'Neill, "Sotomayor Learned the Ropes on the Tarzan Case," *CNN.com,* July 28, 2009, <http://www.cnn.com/2009/US/07/16/sotomayor.district.attorney/index.html?iref=topnews>. Retrieved February, 2015.

CHAPTER 8. LEARNING TO SALSA

1. Sonia Sotomayor. *My Beloved World* (New York: Knopf Publishing, 2013), p. 238.
2. Ibid., p. 272.
3. Neil A. Lewis. "On a Supreme Court Prospect's Resume: Baseball Savior," *New York Times*, May 14, 2009, <http://www.nytimes.com/2009/05/15/us/15sotomayor.html?_r=0>. Retrieved February, 2015.

CHAPTER 9. A FEDERAL ISSUE

1. "Looking Back at Sotomayor's Baseball Ruling," *National Public Radio,* May 27, 2009, <http://www.npr.org/templates/story/story.php?storyId=104597470>. Retrieved February, 2009.
2. Sean Gregory. "How Sotomayor 'Saved' Baseball," *Time,* May 26, 2009, <http://content.time.com/time/nation/article/0,8599,1900974,00.html>. Retrieved February, 2015.
3. Sheryl Gay Stolberg. "Sotomayor, a Trailblazer and a Dreamer," *New York Times,* May 26, 2009, <http://www.nytimes.com/2009/05/27/us/politics/27websotomayor.html?pagewanted=all&_r=0>.

4. Pace Law School Honorary Degree Acceptance Speech. May 18, 2003.

5. Reynolds Holding, "Sonia Sotomayor: A Look at Obama's Supreme Court Pick," *ABC News,* May 26, 2009, <http://abcnews.go.com/Politics/SoniaSotomayor/story?id=7676754>. Retrieved February, 2015.

6. Pace Law School Honorary Degree Acceptance Speech. May 18, 2003.

CHAPTER 10. SUPREMELY WONDERFUL

1. Sheryl Gay Stolberg. "Sotomayor, a Trailblazer and a Dreamer," *New York Times,* May 26, 2009, <http://www.nytimes.com/2009/05/27/us/politics/27websotomayor.html?pagewanted=all&_r=0>.

2. Lori Fossum, "Female US Supreme Court Justices," *University of Washington School of Law,* September 10, 2010, <http://depts.washington.edu/constday/_resources/female-justices.pdf>. Retrieved February, 2015.

3. Julianne Hing, "Justice Sotomayor's Beautiful Schuette Dissent: 'Race Matters,'" Color Lines, April 23, 2014, <http://colorlines.com/archives/2014/04/justice_sotomayors_beautiful_schuette_dissent_race_matters.html>. Retrieved February, 2015.

4. "Oprah's Next Chapter: The Dating Life of a Supreme Court Justice," *Oprah.com,* n.d., <http://www.oprah.com/own-oprahs-next-chapter/Supreme-Court-Justice-Sonia-Sotomayors-Dating-Life-Video>. Retrieved February, 2015.

5. Oprah Winfrey Network. "An Exciting Moment in Justice Sonia Sotomayor's Life: Oprah's Next Chapter: Oprah Winfrey Network," *YouTube,* March 25, 2013 ,<http://www.youtube.com/watch?v=9iUW84jPCHI>. Retrieved February, 2015.

Glossary

appeal—The process of bringing a ruling by a lower court before a higher court for review.

apprehension—The fear that something bad will soon happen.

aspiration—The hope to achieve or accomplish something.

calculation—The answer to a problem, usually in mathematics or science.

commonwealth—A country that belongs to the United States but still maintains its independence, such as Puerto Rico.

constitution—A body of ideas and principles that form the basis for government.

demographic—Information about the population.

depression—Feelings of sadness and hopelessness.

diabetes—A disease that affects the body's ability to produce insulin.

enlist—To sign up or join.

evidence—Facts that prove something.

felony—A serious crime that has a harsher punishment than a misdemeanor.

influence—Being able to have an effect on someone or something.

infraction—An offense that is not as serious as a misdemeanor or a felony; also called a petty crime or violation.

justice—Fair behavior or treatment.

migration—Movement from one area to another.

misdemeanor—A crime that is not as serious as a felony and carries a lighter sentence.

mock trial—A fake trial done by law students as practice.

mythology—A collection of fictional stories belonging to a certain culture or religion.

objectively—Analyzing something without bias or judgment.

pulpit—A raised stand where the preacher speaks to the people.

quota system—A system that requires schools or employers to admit or hire a certain number of minorities.

tenement—An apartment complex usually found in a poorer neighborhood.

white-collar crime— Nonviolent crime motivated by money; involving banking, stocks, and fraud; and committed by middle and upper-class professionals.

wobbler—A charge that can be classified as a misdemeanor or a felony by the prosecutor.

Further Reading

Books

Bernier-Grand, Carmen and Gonzalez, Thomas. *Sonia Sotomayor: Supreme Court Justice.* Tarryton, N.Y.: Marshal Cavenshish Publishing, 2010.

McElroy, Tucker Lisa. *Sonia Sotomayor: First Hispanic US Supreme Court Justice.* Minneapolis, Minn.: Lerner Publications, 2010.

Van Tol, Alex. *Sonia Sotomayor: US Supreme Court Justice.* New York: Crabtree Publishing, 2010.

Winter, Jonah and Rodriguez, Edel. *Sonia Sotomayor: A Judge Grows in the Bronx.* New York: Atheneum Books for Young Readers, 2009.

Web Sites

supremecourt.gov/about/biographies.aspx

The official Web site of the Supreme Court of the United States features biographies of current justices.

whitehouse.gov/the_press_office/Background-on-Judge-Sonia-Sotomayor

Read more about Sonia Sotomayor's background on the White House Web site.

oyez.org/justices/sonia_sotomayor

The Oyez Project at Chicago-Kent College of Law at the Illinois Institute of Technology provides details on Sotomayor's cases.

Index